Thread

A Memoir in Woven Poems

by

Janet McMillan Rives

Finishing Line Press
Georgetown, Kentucky

Thread

A Memoir in Woven Poems

Copyright © 2024 by Janet McMillan Rives
ISBN 979-8-88838-562-3 First Edition
All rights reserved under International and Pan-American Copyright Conventions. No part of this book may be reproduced in any manner whatsoever without written permission from the publisher, except in the case of brief quotations embodied in critical articles and reviews.

Publisher: Leah Huete de Maines
Editor: Christen Kincaid
Cover Art: Kim McNealy Sosin
Author Photo: Kim McNealy Sosin
Cover Design: Kim McNealy Sosin

Order online: www.finishinglinepress.com
also available on amazon.com

Author inquiries and mail orders:
Finishing Line Press
PO Box 1626
Georgetown, Kentucky 40324
USA

Contents

1. Keep Searching 1
2. Snow Day 3
3. Fathers and Daughters 6
4. First Steps 8
5. On the Path 10
6. Reflection 12
7. In Paris 14
8. Thread 16
9. Just Lingering 18
10. Blaze 20
11. Failure 22
12. Lifted 24
13. Restoration 26
14. At the Sandoz Place 28
15. Called to Stay 30
16. Thistle 32
17. Travelers 34
18. For Tomorrow 36
19. Ahead 38

In memory of my sister

Jamie Lynn McMillan

Keep Searching

> After her husband and her mother died the same year,
> the year of my first birthday and her fifty-third,

I never thought about my grandmother's double loss in 1945 until I read the headstones on a visit to Evergreen Cemetery, the resting place of my sister, my parents, grandmother, grandfather, great grandmother, and great aunt. My grandmother and five siblings had come with their widowed mother from Kentucky to Tucson in 1902. She married my grandfather in 1913, so she was still quite young when he died shortly after her mother's death. He had always been a "railroad man" with the Southern Pacific, starting as a surveyor and finishing as an engineer on the run from Tucson east to El Paso and west to Yuma. During the period when he worked as a fireman on a steam engine, filling the firebox with fuel, there was an explosion and my grandfather swallowed "live steam." This event, the family conjectured, was the source of stomach cancer which brought his life to an end at age fifty-six. His obituary suggests age 58, but I heard that he had lied about his age when he was a kid so that he could start working in his mid teens.

> my grandmother began using her railroad pass
> to cross the country and visit us at our home in New England,
> the second floor apartment in a farmhouse
> owned by the university and surrounded by barns.

We had moved into the apartment in 1944 when the entire faculty, it seemed, lived in university-owned housing. Some of my friends lived in Rainbow Alley, tenement style apartments painted bright colors to disguise the shabby construction. Others lived in Quonset huts which had been erected during the war. Did we ever luck out by living next to the horse barn, in front of the cow and pig barns, down the hill from the chickens. It was like living on a farm with none of the chores. How we had the good luck to live in the farmhouse on Horsebarn Hill was a matter of someone else's bad luck. In the summer of 1944, the Hartford circus fire took 167 lives including the agricultural college dean and his wife who lived in the farmhouse. They had attended the circus with their grandson, the dean's secretary, and her daughter. All five perished in the fire. The university sectioned the house into two apartments, one upstairs and one downstairs. By the fall of 1944 when I was six months old, we began our nine year stay upstairs.

> Grandmother's blindness never limited our adventures.
> If she came in winter, we'd belly flop on the sled
> and careen down the hill, me yelling from my perch on top:
> *steer, Grandma, steer,* as we sailed toward the maple.
> If she came in summer, we'd put a dime in an empty Chiclet box,
> a yellow one, and hide it in a stone wall
> on the hill up beyond the horse barn.

That's the thing. I barely knew she was blind. How would I? She did everything with me short of reading a book—played ball, played cards, played dolls, taught me to iron. She wasn't afraid to board a train alone in Tucson, Arizona and disembark days later in Hartford, Connecticut. She sought out adventure, was happy to travel and make discoveries. She told stories and, most important of all, she developed and maintained connections with people. I look back today and realize the ways in which I have followed her example. I have traveled to Europe many times and once to China; I've moved for my education, for job changes and in retirement. Through all of that, I've stayed close to family and old friends while creating connections with people in new places. And I've tried to practice one more lesson from my grandmother: Never give up.

> On her next summer visit we'd search for the dime.
> We never did find the right wall or the right stone,
> but we kept on hiding dimes and we kept on searching for them.
> More than anything else, that's what she taught me to do.

Snow Day

> Icy air seeps under ill-fitted windows
> through which I see nothing but white—
> no maple tree, no stone wall,
> no church steeple, just pure white.

Actually two maple trees graced our yard. The one out front by the road was large, symmetrical, lovely. Depending on the season, it could be loaded with crimson leaves or with little helicopter pods which we'd break open and stick on our noses. The other maple was close to the house by my sister's and my bedroom window. It was for climbing, something I tried to do for years before I succeeded. The stone wall was up the hill next to Route 195. It was the home of my three imaginary friends: Cincy, See Cloud, and Pobby Gellart. Storrs Congregational Church stood across the road from the stone wall. The church was originally built in 1745, and there were headstones out back to prove it. This was our church, a social hub of town as were Saint Thomas Aquinas and Hillel Synagogue just down the road. On a snowy day in February, I could see none of these childhood landmarks.

> Bowls of cornflakes sit on our red
> Chromecroft dinette table
> while Mother stands at the sink,
> cigarette and Coke in hand.

After twenty years of smoking two packs a day of unfiltered Chesterfields, Mother finally gave up cigarettes cold turkey. Her story was that she found herself alone one winter day, husband at out-of-town meetings, three feet of snow in the driveway, and only seven cigarettes on hand. It was time to quit. My story is that my parents were at the early stages of building the first house they would ever own. The smell of stale smoke may have been okay in a rented apartment; but my mother, a neat freak, did not want that stench in her new home.

> We listen to the Bob Steele show
> on WTIC from Hartford, listen
> as the Down Homers' country twang

Country twang in Connecticut? I've come to realize that it's not about north versus south or east versus west, it's about urban versus rural. WTIC served many small communities in the eastern part of the state and played music appropriate to a region where square dancing was a big deal. Adults belonged to square dance clubs and so did kids. I was one of eight children in my class (four boys, four girls) who danced all winter long in each other's living rooms. In spring, at the big festival on campus, we dressed in matching outfits and stole the show. I had two 78 rpm records—Tex Ritter's "Big Rock Candy Mountain" and Prokofiev's "Peter and the Wolf"—and to this day still love both country and classical music.

> is interrupted by a reading
> of school closings: Tolland, Ashford,
> Coventry, Manchester, Willimantic,

Each of those towns was important to me: Tolland, where I attended 4-H camp; Ashford, home of new friends who joined us for high school; Coventry, where I took art lessons; Manchester, where we stopped for lunch at Shady Glen on the way to Hartford; and Willimantic, eight miles from home and the source of everything important—groceries, shoes, toys, school supplies, movies, ice cream sodas.

> then finally, oh joy,
> our Storrs Grammar School.

The grammar school was at the opposite end of town from our rented farmhouse apartment, so a bus ride was required. That might have been scary at first except that my big sister, two years older, was always paving the way. First grade was filled with friends I'd had since nursery school—Brenda, Priscilla, Jono, Ricky—and with a wonderful teacher, Mrs. Gray, who taught us to read. Mrs. Hotchkiss took over in second grade and Mrs. Morris in third. That was the year the girls in my class got in trouble for devising a playground game we called "Catch the Boys and Kiss Them." Mrs. Morris put a quick end to that. Fourth grade was the best with Miss McArthur who wrote original plays in which we starred. In one of them, I was Raggedy Ann and Brenda was Raggedy Andy. By fifth grade, school took a serious turn with Mr. DePalma teaching us how to diagram sentences. The following year Mr. LaVallee taught us the usual array of subjects plus chess. Through those years we trudged each noon to the lunch room for such delicacies as creamed chipped beef on toast, something I've not tasted since. I am convinced the Storrs Grammar School building, the teachers, and my classmates are why I spent my working life in a classroom. In those early years I had no idea I would become a teacher. I only knew it when

I did it, in graduate school and then only to earn some money. Early on I might have guessed reporter or writer; later I would have predicted translator or international economist. Not teacher. But it was in college classrooms that I found the same nurturing, comfort, challenges, and excitement as at Storrs Grammar School.

  Hooray!
  Snow day!

  Even for someone who loved school as much as I did, a snow day was a welcome break, a day to play cards, draw pictures, bake cookies, and build a snow fort.

Fathers and Daughters

*in memory of Óscar Alberto Martinez
and his daughter, Angie Valeria*

> I help Dad load two inner tubes
> into our 'forty-nine Ford.

My father was no mechanic. I guess that's why we got a new car every two years; that way there wasn't enough time for something to go wrong with the old one. We didn't have money so it seems strange to me, a woman who keeps a car for at least ten years, that we bought new cars so frequently. But my father was a marketing professor and a frugal immigrant Scotsman; he must have known what he was doing.

> We are heading to Pine Woods Pond
> on this warm June Saturday.
> Mother and Jamie have better things to do.
> But what could be better than this?

I say "Pine Woods Pond" because it sounds good. It was really Diana's Pool near my hometown of Storrs in rural Connecticut. Though Diana's Pool was hidden in the woods, it was always crowded with families and with students from the college. Often my father and I would find things like this to do that did not include my mother and sister, usually sports of some kind.

> I am still little, not a good swimmer
> but I am not afraid.
> Dad can swim. He helps me
> learn to dog paddle.

Dad was good at every sport having played most of them at Bowen High School in Chicago's south side in the 1920s. He excelled at basketball (on the "lightweight" team), baseball, tennis, and golf. He continued to play those sports until age forty when he declared, "No more running sports." Then it was just golf, a game he taught me with joy and patience, a game which kept us bonded forever.

> Dad teaches me something every day,
> about swimming, about words,
> about telling the truth.

He taught me my first poem, "Little Boy Blue," by Eugene Field, a poem I memorized when I was five. And he taught me his favorite poem, "If," by Rudyard Kipling. Both of these are in my very old copy of *One Hundred and One Famous Poems*, a book I keep at hand. Dad helped me to write my own poems, silly poems, rhyming poems, limericks. He taught me to be honest, to keep a trust. If I said, "Dad, please don't tell Mother," he wouldn't.

> After we splash and kick,
> stretch out on the flat rock,
> talk about baseball and ice cream,
> we float on our backs,
> look up at the sky.

My childhood overflowed with freedom and delight. I can see myself then, that little girl who spent hours in the yard throwing a ball against the front steps so that it would careen back in some crazy way. She would hit a ball straight up in the air, drop the bat, grab her glove and catch the white sphere before it could hit the ground. Only when she intercepted her father, before he could make it inside the house after work, would the real baseball game begin. Besides sharing the money he earned (we always had enough, never too much), my father shared his time, his passions, adventures, expertise. He never missed family dinners during which he recounted his day and made room for the women in his family to share their stories and opinions.

But why am I thinking of my father so much today? Here is the reason. Last night as I checked the news on my laptop, I came across a photo of a man and his young daughter, migrants, lying face down in the Rio Grande River during a harrowing trip from El Salvador. Her hand is tucked inside his tee shirt, her arm around his neck. Óscar and Angie. A father and daughter at the water's edge.

First Steps

> Second grade
> In a southwest city
> my first city

I'm halfway through second grade and we've come to stay with Grandma in Arizona. Daddy's taking some kind of vacation from his job, but he doesn't want me to call it a vacation. I'm supposed to say sabbatical. It took us a long time to drive here in our Ford, but Jamie and I stayed busy in the back seat with games, puzzles, and trying to be the first to see a white horse. We got up in the dark on the day we left and saw a man walking a black horse from the barn up the hill right past our house. It was Andy, the horse I rode on Saturdays before we came here.

> first time walking to school,
> no bus,
> first time walking home for lunch

Last year when I started first grade, I had to walk up the hill and wait for a yellow school bus to take me to Storrs Grammar School. And I ate hot lunch at school. Here in Tucson, Grandma's house is at 707 North Euclid Avenue. It's where Mother lived until she finished college and married Daddy. Then they moved to Iowa and then Chicago and then Connecticut where I'm from. My school here is Roskruge Elementary and it's on Sixth Street between Third and Fourth Avenues. I memorized the streets the day Grandma walked us to school.

> a nickel from Grandma
> pressed into my hand
> to buy a candy bar
> at the corner drug store

Sometimes it's a Milky Way and sometimes M & M's. Grandma is so nice to give me money for candy after she makes me a bologna sandwich. And she plays Go Fish with me and tells me scary ghost stories.

> first corner drug store

The drug store is in the Geronimo Hotel just up the block. Grandma says to walk all the way to the corner before I cross the street. We don't have a drug store at home, no stores at all. Everyone thinks that's funny because the name of our town is Storrs.

There's lots do in Grandma's town. Next week we're going to the rodeo. Daddy took me shopping for some real Levi's and a cowboy shirt. It has red and black squares on it like a checkerboard. And he promised to buy me boots, too. Sometimes after school, Jamie and I go to our cousin Joanne's house. She and David just had a baby. She is really cute but cries a lot. They live near Roskruge, right near the corner whey we buy cups of shaved ice with syrup on it. Mother told me what it's called, but I can't remember. Oh, and last week we drove up the mountains and discovered a place called Sabino Canyon. We wore our bathing suits and splashed in the water. Mother said that's what she used to do when she was little.

I can't wait to go to school on Monday. I like my teacher and I've already made some friends.

first black friend

Her name is Janet Green. I've never met anyone with my same name before. I think we are going to be best friends.

first brown friend

Danny Robles is so cute. Sometimes I follow him home from school but I stay behind so he won't notice me. But I really want to be his friend.

first steps into the world.

On the Path

> I wake to the smell of Mother's coffee
> to the sound of Deuce barking next door
> to the taste of anticipation.

Mother drinks coffee now instead of Coke. And she doesn't smoke anymore, thank goodness. And oh, dogs. I was always afraid of the Young's dog. They lived downstairs in the farmhouse we just left. I'm not sure I understand what "renting" means exactly, but I know one thing—this is OUR house. We've watched it be built, seen it grow every single day. We will keep it clean, the yard too, we promise. And now I have neighbors and dogs, too, dogs that are gentle and sweet, Deuce and Betsy's dog Honey.

> Our house emits the tang of new construction.
> I glow with excitement for new neighbors,
> a new teacher, a new way to school.

Almost every day Dad's been bringing me here after work so we can smell it, see where my bedroom will be (my very own bedroom for just me), meet our neighbors—the Bartholomews, the Johnsons, the Gants, the Deans. I know I'm grinning, but I'm so happy. I can feel myself blushing; my freckles are popping off my cheeks. Oh, wow. I suddenly have so many kids to play with and so does Jamie, kids our age and younger ones too. I'm nine, going into fourth grade in just three weeks. Miss McArthur will be my teacher; yes, the teacher Jamie loved so much two years ago. Best of all, no more bus to school. I can walk there with my friends.

> When Betsy, Jane, and I cross the Gants' backyard
> the woods await us. We discover the path.
> As if we'd entered a cathedral, our giddy girl talk calms.

What are these trees anyway? There are more here than just the maples and pines we had at the apartment, more colors and shapes, more smells. My friends are like body guards on this walk. I am on my own for sure, but they protect me, keep me company.

> Sticks crack beneath our shoes, leaves brush our shoulders,
> fresh welcoming scents take our breath away.
> We begin to walk with reverence.

I'm just a kid, excited for school, a new pencil box from Woolworth's to put in my desk, a ham sandwich and cookies in my lunch box. I wonder: Will I remember these days when I'm an old lady? Will I remember Connecticut autumns, jumping in a leaf pile in Bart's front yard, stealing Macintosh apples from the orchard up on Hillside Circle, pressing crimson maple leaves between sheets of waxed paper, rescuing a robin's egg fallen from the nest, running the bases of our make-shift street field, setting off firecrackers in the Johnson's backyard, whispering to Bobby standing below my bedroom window on a Friday night. Will I remember? Or will it all be fuzzy, forgotten?

Reflection

> *"If you look at a glass, you will eventually find there—if you let your imagination and memory inhabit it—all that you know and care about."* Robert Pinsky

> This small rock reflects mixed colors
> but mostly gray like our house in New England

The house was, more precisely, in rural eastern Connecticut. Gray sided with white shutters, it was newly constructed and the first my parents had owned.

> behind which stood Ingalls Rock
> where I learned the art of kissing.

It was a large granite rock located at the back edge of the lot next door where Mr. and Mrs. Ingalls and their twin sons lived in a white house with black shutters. He was the football coach, and the boys were my first baby sitting charges. At first, I baby sat only during the day, earning twenty-five cents an hour. Oh, and the kissing. That happened a few years later when my neighbor, Betsy, and our "boyfriends," Tony and Jono, would climb onto Ingalls Rock. We'd heard about spin the bottle but didn't have one so, instead, we used Tony's "Family Shellfish Permit." It spun beautifully and so did we.

> This rock could have been from the collection
> we found in the attic at Horsebarn Hill
> or I might have picked it up on the trip
> to New Hampshire with my earth science class

I was a freshman in high school when the new junior-senior high was opened. Students from Storrs no longer had to take the bus to Windham High School eight miles away. Kids from my neighborhood could walk to school in no more than ten minutes. Earth science was a class for freshmen. I wish I could say I loved it, but no. I did love the weekend class trip to New Hampshire, camping out and collecting rocks with twenty other fourteen year olds.

> or when my family stopped at Frog Rock
> on our way to the beach in Rhode Island.

There were so many trips to water in those days: Sullivan's Pond, Diana's Pool, Ocean Beach, Mashamoquet. The best was Misquamicut in Westerly, Rhode Island, just over the state line. I never liked to swim (still don't), but I loved running in the waves and building castles with the fine, soft sand. The greatest joy, both going and coming home, was the sight of Frog Rock in Eastford, Connecticut, the perfect place for a picnic.

> There's red in this rock, a deeper crimson
> than the Catalina Mountains
> as they stretch toward Mexico
> reflecting the setting sun.

Those childhood places are so far from where I sit today at my writing desk in southern Arizona, the tips of the north face of the Santa Catalina Mountains barely in view. There is "far" counted in miles and years, and there is "far" counted in memories.

> I touch the rock and notice
> little flecks of mica glittering, shiny
> like the mica we'd pick off and flick
> into the crisp autumn air.

I probably learned about mica in earth science class or even before when I examined my rock collection. If there is a season from my youth that I carry with me, it is fall. I am sitting on Ingalls Rock with Betsy and the boys after school one Thursday in October. We've all ridden our bikes here from school, such freedom, such promise. Like mica we float away in the crisp autumn air.

> Before I drop it where I found it,
> with the Iowa river rock lining the walkway,
> I see how small it is, tiny in fact but solid
> like a memory I cannot crush even if I try.

In Paris

> When I was young
> they put me in this city
> on these famous streets
> among these gigantic monuments.

It certainly wasn't my idea to spend eighth grade in Paris, away from my friends, from my first boyfriend, from the town and school and neighborhood I loved. But I had no vote, so off we went, a family of four, not one of us speaking a single word of French. The night we arrived after seven days crossing the Atlantic and then a long train ride from Le Havre, a taxi took us to the Hotel Regina at Place des Pyramides. There she was, Joan of Arc in bronze, triumphant astride her horse, banner raised high. That was the first Paris monument I saw, one of many I would come to adore. My favorite, always, was the Eiffel Tower, especially seen from below. Next favorite was a small replica of the Statue of Liberty situated on a small island, l'Ile des Cygnes, in the Seine near where I lived during my junior year in college. Another favorite, the steeple of the American Church on Quai d'Orsay might not be considered a monument per se, but I have always loved its welcoming presence.

> They put words in my mouth,
> words that slipped out
> without pain
> without difficulty.
> My days were normal;
> I breathed easily.

It was the wrong Hotel Regina that first night, by the way. The taxi driver eventually delivered us to the Regina de Passy, the correct hotel, more modest lodging on the rue de la Tour. That's where Fritz, the German night clerk who spoke perfect American English thanks to a stint in a POW camp in Pittsburgh, put some French words in my mouth. The words, let me translate, were: "Four ham sandwiches without butter and four Cokes, if you please." We used those words at the *tabac* down the street and had our first Parisian meal at ten p.m. on a September night in 1957. That was the beginning of my lifelong connection to all things French, an infatuation with the French language, a love that translated into two more years in France. Yes, during both those years my days were normal. As a junior in college studying at the Sorbonne, I concentrated on my studies, realizing that the A grade attained at home was destined to become a perfectly acceptable 14 points out of 20 in France. And as a young professor in Dijon, I juggled teaching and research with buying food and maintaining an apartment. Nothing could have been more normal.

> But in coming back today,
> forty years later,
> everything seems big
> fantastic
> special.
> I am wordless,
> breathless.

Since the last year I lived in France, now over forty-four years ago, I have returned many times as a tourist. I am bonded to the old places: our apartment in Sèvres, the Bois de Boulogne where our school was located, the American Church, the apartment near Pont Mirabeau, the Sorbonne, Luxembourg Garden, rue Vavin on the other side of the Garden. Yet I always search for new adventures: the Museum of the Arab World, a hotel on the right rather than the left bank, a walk along the Canal Saint-Martin. Somehow this connection to Paris seems an odd fit, completely out of character. The city is glamorous; I am not. It's noisy; I like quiet. Paris is bustling; I prefer a slower pace. Could my attachment to Paris have something to do with facing a challenge at an early age, learning to live in a strange place and speak a foreign language? Or maybe it is the memory of shared experiences with family, newness and familiarity all at once.

Decades ago I learned that the Swiss composer Arthur Honegger had the idea for the opening theme of his symphony number 4, *Deliciae Basiliensis*, while riding on bus 92 between Place de l'Etoile and Alma. I realize that if I were to hop on bus 82 and ride from one end of the line to the other, I could see almost all of the places that meant something to me during eighth grade, during my junior year of college, and when I visited Paris monthly during my year in Dijon. Yes, riding bus 82 is my plan for the next trip to Paris. It might leave me wordless, breathless. Or it might be an inspiration for a symphony or, more realistically, for a poem.

Thread

>I hold the thread next to the pants I'm about to hem,
>both of them the same soft brown, the color
>of a childhood skirt, my 4-H project. On the top
>*Star Mercerized 19 cents.*

My hometown was just rural enough to support several 4-H clubs. I'm always hesitant to say I was a 4-H'er; it sounds as though I may have been raising cattle or goats. Hardly. Our first club (The Whip-Poor-Wills) was all girls and led by Mrs. Passmore. We involved ourselves with nature—bird watching, making Christmas wreaths, growing flowers. The subsequent club, the same girls with Mrs. Fisher as our leader, was a sewing group. In both clubs, I served as the "reporter." One of my short pieces would occasionally appear in the *Willimantic Chronicle*.

>Goodness, this is the thread
>from my skirt, its tender filaments connecting me
>to a little city that sparked my fascination with places
>that were once so much more than they are today,
>a city that spawned my dreams of adventure,
>that made me contemplate commerce, manufacturing,
>language, culture, travel.

That little city, Willimantic, was eight miles from my town. I say "city," but I see that the population of Willi never exceeded 13,000 during the years we lived in Connecticut. That might sound like a small town, but Willi was a city to us. Willi was where we bought our groceries at the A & P store, where we saw Dr. Fox our dentist, bought Stride Rite shoes, visited Mr. Roan at his tire and appliance store, ate a rare meal in a fancy restaurant, had an ice cream soda at Hallock's. It was where I hung around as my mother looked for clothes at Tubridy's and where she hung around while I perused Woolworth's school supply aisles.

>In its heyday, Willimantic welcomed immigrants,
>Irish, Italian, Polish, French Canadian.
>Throughout the last century they came from Estonia,
>Latvia, Ukraine, Puerto Rico. They came to work
>in the looming gray stone monument by the river,
>the *American Thread Company*, the exact words
>I now see on the bottom of this spool of thread.

Willimantic was a complex and interesting place, especially when compared to our homogenous college town. I could walk down Main Street in Willi and hear half a dozen foreign languages, visit a variety of specialty stores. We could drive by busy factories and see all sorts of housing from mansions to crowded apartment buildings. I wonder if my early exposure to Willi had something to do with my college majors, Economics and French. Perhaps my early trips to this industrial and commercial center influenced my choice of career as an economics professor or had something to do with my continued love of foreign languages, my tendency to read books by immigrant writers. In Willimantic I saw possibilities for a life of discovery, visiting new places, hearing fresh voices, learning about new cultures. My childhood wonder inspired by this single place, led me to adult choices which have shaped my life.

> How I long to go back to that city, back to see
> Victorian homes still crowding Prospect Hill,
> back to the Capitol Theater, restored to the magical
> palace of my youth, back to discover the new statue,
> a frog sitting on a spool of thread, the very thread
> I hold in my hand today.

Just Lingering

*"Such gifts, bestowed,
can't be repeated."* Mary Oliver

>I made my way home after school
>and after whatever came after school,
>basketball practice, perhaps, student council,

One of the best things about going to a small high school was having the chance to be part of every activity we chose to pursue. And the best part of living within walking distance of school was not depending on parents for transportation.

>field hockey, yes, probably a fall sport
>because I remember the day as Indian summer,
>maples draped in their crimson jackets,
>me with a red sweater tied around my waist,
>walking in reverie, lost in daydreams.

Fall. What could be better than a warm autumn day in New England? Peak color in northeast Connecticut was generally the second week in October so, yes, field hockey would be what we were playing. School dismissed early, two-thirty or so, but I never made it home till almost dinner time. Crisp days were my favorites, but that one warm fall day, a throwback to August, was a pleasant surprise in its own way. The dry air brought out the smell of leaves underfoot; the pale blue sky soothed school-rattled nerves.

>Then I heard your voice behind me, you
>calling out for me to stop, wait up.

There were so many voices calling to me in those days. Johnny, who lived two doors up the street, had been my friend long before we were neighbors, probably starting when our older sisters became best friends in first grade. Johnny was the brother I never had, a confidant, the man who would call me in the middle of a pandemic sixty years after high school just to make sure I wasn't becoming too socially distant. Betsy lived in the house behind mine and was the quintessential best friend, partner in crime, keeper of secrets, the person I would call in the middle of a pandemic to make sure she was keeping her good humor intact. Jane, from next door, was one year younger, not enough to keep the strongest bonds from forming, tying us together like the pulley system we rigged to carry notes in code between our houses. Bobby was the boy from across the street, first love from junior high on. Each of these friends at one time or another called me to stop, wait up.

> We sat for a long time on a log by the brook,
> spoke about the lovely day, our place in the world,
> the order of things, not teenage banter
> but words we used like tools to carve an image
> of the two of us lingering that autumn afternoon,

Images are as clear today as ever: Me playing basketball with Johnny in his basement on a snowy day; Betsy retrieving *Peyton Place* from under her bed to read me the marked passages; Jane teaching me the Hail Mary during a sleepover at her house; Bobby throwing pebbles at my bedroom window after dark. My friends, I will always wait up for you, always share these images of us.

> sitting still for just a second of our long and lucky lives.

Blaze

>Every day dull

That is precisely what I thought last fall when we moved to this dusty city in the Sonoran Desert. I've been here half a year and desperately miss my Connecticut woods, the grass, the red leaves in fall, dark tree trunks outlined against snow. How am I ever going to learn to love subtle?

>then suddenly
>from within the flat tan
>emerge such gems:

A few weeks ago, my parents talked me into going with them on a drive through wildflower territory. We live on the Tucson side of the Santa Catalina Mountains where I can gaze at Finger Rock from my bedroom window. Someone just told me that's what the rock formation is called; to me, it's just been "My Castle." We took Skyline Drive and Ina Road west to Oracle Road and headed north to Oracle Junction. Once we got to the "back side" of the Catalinas, I told my parents that the mountains look dark and foreboding, not welcoming like our side. But my mother insists that, from all directions, they are "startlingly beautiful"— her words, not mine.

We headed north on Highway 79, officially named Pinal Pioneer Parkway but known to my family as Tom Mix highway. Somewhere along the route to Florence they showed me a monument dedicated to the cowboy actor who was killed there in an automobile accident in 1940. Tom Mix Highway is famous for wildflowers. My mother, born and raised in Tucson and a gardener, sure knows her stuff. She identified all of them—Mexican gold poppies, blue Mojave lupine, yellow desert marigolds, orange globe mallow. I have to admit that even in our yard in the Foothills we can see color.

>the turquoise underside
>of a desert lizard,
>flaming jasper
>on barrel cacti

Little by little I am beginning to relish calm desert tones—blue green agave, muted orchid skies at sunrise, subtle pink reflecting off the mountain side, cool cloudless azure skies throughout this past winter. And now that spring is here, I have discovered how subtle becomes explosive.

yellow palo verde
gone to topaz.
Look!
Our desert's
ablaze.

Failure

> Failure was something to be avoided
> by a fifties' kid coming of age
> in a decade when the world
> was perfectly fine
> every family compatible, stable
> every town a Lake Wobegon
> every person following The Plan.

Mine was an idyllic childhood, sort of fifties fake like my friends' lives. The one bump in the road was the move from Connecticut to Arizona at age 16, a boulder actually. I adjusted poorly to the dusty city, large high school, isolated neighborhood, really no neighborhood at all. There was no hanging out after school watching American Bandstand, no impromptu baseball games in the middle of the street, no walking to school through the woods. We had one tree in our yard, a eucalyptus; there was nothing else but cactus and scruffy bushes.

> Failure during college in the sixties
> was a girl who didn't get good grades
> didn't join a sorority, didn't walk to class
> with a pack of friends   *hi guys*
> didn't wear Lanz dresses
> and Capezios from the College Shop
> didn't go out on a date
> every single Saturday night.
> I was not a failure.

When *okay* follows *really bad,* it seems like *great.* I completely bought into college life those first two years at the University of Arizona. But my junior year in Paris heralded a new phase: high heels, chignon hair-do, books of poetry, plays and operas, perfecting my French. I borrowed "style" from Madame Beaulieu, professor of geography. I feigned knowledge of the world thanks to Monsieur Duverger, professor of political science. My college days pretty much ended when I returned to the U of A, devoting my senior year to a serious preparation for graduate studies in economics. A boyfriend in another state minimized distractions of campus dating, drinking, partying. Most nights I was off to the Science Library to crack the books: money and banking, international trade, economic development, calculus. And so it continued into grad school.

> But then came the post college
> "must do," time to get married.
> Failure (for him too) was choosing
> the wrong mate, compromising
> on a job, living in the wrong place
> and oh no, getting divorced.

Imagine a young woman, unhappy, embarrassed, not knowing where to turn, unsure of her next step. Picture me sitting in a car outside the post office near Glen Riddle, Pennsylvania where we lived, fiddling with my wedding ring, wondering when I would take it off for good. There I was rehearsing a call to my parents when I would tell them Bill had moved out, and soon they would be parents to two divorced daughters. I was never more alone than then. I wondered, "How did this ever happen." Oh, I moved on, but it took time for me to come to my senses.

> Then came career, college teaching,
> travel, vibrant family dinners
> with nieces and cousins,
> outdoor concerts on clear desert days,
> poems and books shared with friends.
> Wait! Was that really failure so long ago
> or was it the start of finding what counts?

Lifted

> A long walk north
> through the *Jardin de Luxembourg*
> around the *Grand Basin*
> the bullet riddled *Palais*
> the statue of Minerva
> a tiny owl in her hand

I took this walk so many times during the year I lived in Dijon at age thirty. I was teaching at the École Supérieure de Commerce in Dijon and doing research on the topic "The Role of Women in the French Economy." It was the United Nations Year of the Woman, 1974. Research was my excuse for going to Paris for one week each month, either driving my leased baby blue Renault Cinq and parking it for the duration of my stay or, much easier, taking the train.

I was already very familiar with the Jardin de Luxembourg from the year I spent as a college junior studying at the Sorbonne. The Jardin was the perfect hangout, the spot for a picnic lunch or a nap, if I didn't mind paying a small fee to the woman who supervised the benches. I loved seeing the statue of Minerva holding an owl, the official "symbol" of my college sorority. As for bullet riddled buildings, I had read much about Paris during World War II and was always taken aback by the placards on buildings noting who had been killed on that very spot or signs at train stations indicating how many people had been sent to concentration camps.

When I have returned to Paris in the years since I lived in Dijon, my level of comfort has been surprising. There is never a period of transition, no feeling of displacement, unless you count the few days my lips and jaws hurt from making the switch from English to French.

> then across the Seine
> into the shadow
> of Notre Dame.

My love of Notre Dame dates back to the days when I was in eighth grade living with my family in Sèvres. We would play tourist on Sundays after the morning service at the American Church of Paris on Quai d'Orsay. My mother, armed always with her green Michelin Guide, would provide the history lessons. I can still picture Napoléon placing a crown on his head in front of the altar of Notre Dame.

> Inside I found a chair
> near the transept
> where delicate harmonies
> of a boys' choir
> closed my eyes.

During one particular trip to Paris, in the late eighties to present a paper at an economics conference, my friends and I combatted our fatigue after our transatlantic flight by taking an enormously long walk through the Jardin de Luxembourg all the way to the Notre Dame. I was beat.

> When I woke
> and made my way
> back up the aisle
> toward the entrance
> of that somber magnificence,
> sunlight streaming through
> blue red green glass
> arose within me.

Television shots of Notre Dame burning on April 15, 2019 drew me back to that long walk and the coolness of the cathedral. Now it is cinders. I can only pray that Notre Dame will be restored, that this particular connection I have to Paris will not be lost. I have not been back to Paris since Notre Dame burned, and I can't wait to return. I long to speak French, to be immersed in a city, country, culture, society and geography that seem to fit me so well. I look forward being in a place which has always lifted me.

Restoration

"First prize, Exterior Rehabilitation, One-Ten,
One-Twelve Linden Street, Camden."

When I saw the magazine photograph in 1992, the flashback was immediate. The house was gorgeous, but its address told me it had not always looked like this.

> The row house is like so many
> I walked past, day after day,
> abandoned
> so far inside myself, I could never
> see green glass among the cinders,

I tore the page from my magazine and added a short note saying, "I probably walked by this place a million times." That would have been during my first job after graduate school. It was 1970, a time of marriage and compromise. Mine was taking a teaching job at Rutgers University's branch campus in Camden, New Jersey. Thinking my time there would be short—just enough for my husband to finish a two-year post doc an hour away—I accepted a job at a school from which I could easily move, or so I thought. Even I, an economist, was unable to predict the poor job market for professors in the mid 1970s.

Rutgers had chosen a spot dead center in the worst part of north Camden for its South Jersey branch campus, hoping I suppose that it might help renew a blighted area. It did not. In 1970 the campus consisted of one main building plus the law school. A few years later, an old warehouse, which had belonged to either RCA or Campbell Soup, was retrofitted to become the classroom and office building for the business and economics department. I could barely hear myself talk when the High Speed Line went across the Ben Franklin Bridge next to my classroom. I could barely hear myself for the six years I was there.

> could never imagine the promise
> of repointed brick, pine colored
> posts, rich cream trim.
> I saw only cinders, rotted wood,
> peeling paint, rats.

I put the magazine photograph with my note in a section of a binder labeled "Poem Ideas." It sat there until a day in 2016 when my poetry appreciation group was going to discuss William Carlos Williams. It didn't take long for me to find his poem, "Between Walls." I pictured Camden, remembered the magazine photograph, found it and my note. An idea that lay dormant for twenty-four years was transformed into a finished poem in the span of an hour. I felt cleansed, restored.

> Escape
> to prairie and cornfield,
> a mosaic of lapis, amber, jade
> seasons of renewal.

Some people need the vibrancy of a city to feel alive. For me it's the opposite. I need the calm of a rural setting to sense life fully. I need to hear, see, smell, touch nature. Only in a setting similar to that of my childhood—a place of fields and trees and wildlife—could I be restored and renewed.

At the Sandoz Place

To say that Nebraska surprised me would be an understatement. Nebraska blew me away. I came there from a job I did not like, a marriage that had not worked, and a part of the country with no appeal to me. Nebraska fascinated me with its plains' mix of Midwest and West, its independent bent and its inhabitants who seemed to readily accept anyone willing to live there. I felt more at home there after a day than after years in other places I had lived.

> It takes a hard place to soften the heart.
> It takes icy nights to melt the soul,
> a heavy door closed against the cold
> to open you up enough to let the stranger in,
> sharing the darkest secrets life has left you.

To unravel the mysteries of Nebraska, I set out to read its authors and discovered three favorites: Willa Cather, Mari Sandoz, and Wright Morris. Now I would add a fourth author, poet Ted Kooser, an Iowan by birth but a Nebraskan at heart. As for Willa Cather, I devoured everything she wrote—novels, short stories, essays, memoir, poetry. I admired her ability to capture both landscape and human emotions. I started with *Song of the Lark* and moved on to *Death Comes for the Archbishop, O! Pioneers, My Ántonia, The Professor's House*. I could go on. I read every book and collected most of them, sometimes hardbacks published by Alfred A. Knopf in the 1920s. I visited Cather's house in Red Cloud and was entranced by the bedroom, an exact replica, down to the wallpaper, of what she had described in *Song of the Lark*. I read several books by Mari Sandoz and was especially taken by *Old Jules*, her account of her father who had immigrated from Switzerland to the remote Sandhills of western Nebraska.

> It takes the searing summer sun to cool your fire,
> the relentless wind to calm your pace
> and make you stop and look and love this land,
> love it into what you want it to be,
> something green and growing
> something that will last forever.

On a trip west on Highway 20, a friend and I stopped in Gordon to visit the Mari Sandoz Museum which was housed at the time on the second floor of a furniture store. (The museum now has a new home at Chadron State College.) We asked about the Sandoz homestead and were told to follow

Highway 27 south for thirty miles. If Mari's niece were at home, we heard, she would likely invite us in for tea. We found the homestead, but no one was home. I sat on the warm Nebraska earth near Mari's gravestone and gazed at Jules's orchard blow and thought about Nebraska, remote and welcoming.

> It takes hills that roll along
> in perfect space, without a tree
> to make a man put in the seed
> to make him try and fail, time after time
> till now the fruit abounds, falls to the ground,
> an orchard in all its glory
> too few will ever see.

Called to Stay

"My field unamplified as the voice of one bird's in the corn...." Mona Van Duyn, from "Falls"

> I would have settled
> for the single crop

Corn everywhere. That's all I saw when I first moved to Iowa. Soon I learned Iowa wasn't just full of corn but also soybeans as well as the cattle and pigs that ate feed made from corn and beans.

> would have been thrilled
> to drive the curvy road
> past the Quaker meeting house
> past the horse farm

My driving route from Cedar Falls, where I lived, to Ames where I visited a friend, covered part of the east central portion of the state. I experimented with many highways and county blacktops until I found my favorite. That route contained the prettiest spot of all, a curvy road that stretched along a ridge just south of New Providence in Hardin County. The meeting house was a surprise, not the denomination I'd expected to find in rural Iowa. The sign outside the horse farm read "Clampitt." It must be the family of the renowned poet Amy Clampitt, who came from New Providence but lived her adult life in New York City.

> around the bend
> where the red tailed hawk
> soared above the trees
> left twisted by the spiral wind.

I did see a hawk once on that curve, its tail more orange than red when highlighted against a pale blue sky. I observed the damage from the New Providence tornado just days after it struck.

> The place you left
> is like the place I left,
> the place from which I was taken
> on great adventures,

>   from which I was torn, finally,
>   from my moorings

    As a young girl, Mona Van Duyn moved from Waterloo, Iowa (near where I lived for thirty-four years), to Eldora, just east of New Providence. Her adopted town, like my hometown in Connecticut, was small, a place where one could not hide. Each of us was taken on great adventures, Mona to Yosemite and Niagara Falls, me to Arizona and Paris. She moved as soon as she was able, because Eldora could not contain her. I moved at sixteen because my parents said that's what we were doing. Yet I always longed for the stability of the place where I began.

>   till so much later I dropped anchor
>   into this sea of green
>   and heard your bird
>   call me to stay.

Thistle

> It is the spiky weed that pricks my fingers
> lifting pine cones from the hosta.

Canada thistle is the bane of Iowa flower gardeners, especially those with lovely beds of hosta (plantain lilies). I loved my hosta plants, the tiny ones with variegated leaves, the large "elephant ears" up to five feet in diameter, and especially those with a deep dark green sheen. These showy plants loved the semi shade under my pine trees. Sadly the prickly Canada thistle, such a noxious and invasive weed, also found a home there. When I would remove the thistle, not an easy task given the stubborn root system, it was worth getting pricked just to be able to enjoy the handsome hosta bed beneath the pines.

> It is the purple blossom catching my eye
> as I drive through prairie sandhills.

Spare beauty defines that land in western Nebraska, spare beauty yet beauty to spare. I delighted in living in Omaha during my early career and now relish car trips through the Sandhills. I recently traveled with a friend to a meeting of the Prairie Plains Resource Institute in Harrison just eight miles east of Wyoming. Another trip's purpose was to play golf at the Prairie Club thirty minutes south of Valentine. Some trips had no purpose at all other than to drive on Highway 2 and enjoy the panoramic vistas. Yes, on these trips Canada thistle catches my eye from a safe distance away. I have learned that this weed infests over 450,000 acres in Nebraska and that it was first identified as a noxious weed in 1873. Nebraska farmers and ranchers have been fighting it for a long, long time. But I am more like the butterflies than I am like the farmers: I love the thistles and a million other prairie wildflowers in subtle shades of blue, violet, and rose.

> It is the mauve cluster on the back of my cap,
> Saint Andrew's cross embroidered on the front.

The hat was purchased in a tourist shop in Ayr south of Glasgow and sold to me by, who knows, maybe by a distant or not so distant relative, someone named McMillan or Park or Dempster. I wonder who lives in Aunt Meg's house where my sister and I visited as teenagers and spent our "tuppence" at the local soda shop listening to The Platters on the jukebox. Could it still house family members? Maybe it's the home of one of the second cousins we met on that long ago trip, Andrew and Murray, such handsome lads all decked out in their kilts. I think of relatives I barely knew because an ocean and then a continent separated us. The cross on the front of my hat is a reminder of the flag hanging in the Presbyterian church I attended in Iowa where, on Saint Andrew's Sunday, a man dressed in tartan piped us out of the sanctuary to the tune of "Scotland the Brave." I can picture myself as a young girl memorizing a poem by Robert Burns or singing "You take the high road and I'll take the low road" just the way Grandma Mac taught me.

> It is the silver pendant, the amethyst charm
> suspended close to my heart,

One of them is the shape of a thistle, the other the color. Both are reminders of family still in my heart, some whom I knew in this country, some whom I met in Ayr, some whom I can only imagine.

> It is the source of seeds held in a young man's fist
> as he sails toward Ellis Island.

I see my grandfather standing stalwart on the deck of the S.S. Caledonia, bold and tenacious like his native country's national flower. But maybe he was a little lonely, too, having left his wife and three children at home in Ayr while he explored the possibility of a new life in Chicago. He must have wondered if he would discover opportunities for a better life in America in the second decade of the twentieth century. He must have worried about finding a comfortable, welcoming community for his family of five. He must have hoped they would be accepted, must have believed his children, like a thistle, could grip the soil of this new land and flourish. He must have missed home and the sight of thistle (*clauran* in Scottish Gaelic) covering the hills of the old country.

> It is my father's *clauran* hills the day he is carried
> from his homeland by dreamers.

Travelers

> Brave boy waits
> beside Dongting lake

When I first met Qiu Yu, I was taken by his maturity and by his command of spoken English. It was difficult to believe he'd arrived in the U.S. just two months earlier. He told me he was from a place north of Beijing near a large lake. I pictured a lake in China, not his lake but one I had visited on my trip to China in the early 1980s. Our large travel group, sponsored by the organization Friendship Force, traveled by train from Shanghai to Hangzhou. We spent a day visiting West Lake. What a gorgeous setting—gardens, pagodas, temples, bridges, water lilies. It was clear to me how the beauty and serenity of West Lake had inspired writers and artists since the 9th century.

> Brief breezes
> curve bamboo.
> Reeds ripple water.
> Along banks
> willows rustle.

I felt connected to China almost immediately in much the same way as I feel connected to Qiu Yu. What returns to me after three decades are not images of monuments, not the Forbidden City, not Tiantan Park, not the Great Wall. I remember connections. There was a young Chinese man I tried to speak with in English only to find out he did not know English but had studied French. We spoke of our passion for French in our common tongue, I having learned it by living in France and he by listening to the radio each and every Tuesday night. And I remember the young tour guide who showed us around a glass factory and shared with me that she loved American poets. "Who's your favorite?" I asked. "Robert Frost," she answered. "Mine too," I told her. When I returned home I sent her a paperback book of Frost's poems and received in return a perfectly written thank-you note. These were connections that bridged continents, oceans, age, culture.

> Clouds collect
> against sky in fall.

When I met Qiu Yu last spring and asked how to pronounce his name, he told me that his grandfather had named him and that his name means "sky in fall." As I drove home from the tutoring session, I knew I had to write a poem and knew that it would include an image of the sky in fall. And in that sky, I pictured a migratory bird finding its way home.

I had not seen Qiu Yu since last April, so today I asked the ELD (English Language Development) teacher if he was still in school. She said yes, he would be in her class in one hour. Even though Qiu Yu no longer needs help with reading English, she sent him to my spot in the library. I found out more about him today. His parents divorced when he was four. His mother came to the U.S. "for a better life," but he stayed with his father in China until last year when he was seventeen. Clearly he misses his beautiful homeland, his father, a society and culture which he understands and embraces. Each day in America Qiu Yu drifts further homeward.

>   A lone pied avocet
>   weaves a map
>   from memory.
>   The boy follows.

For Tomorrow

"...it was only the dust in one sunbeam."
W. S. Merwin in "Child Light"

>So much about memory.
>So much about what was.

I write. Mostly I write from memory of the early years shared with my small family, mother, father, sister, all of them gone now. In order to reminisce, to stay connected, I need to write. There is no one left to talk with about events of the past, mostly good moments, some hilarious like the photo of my sister at three, standing in the front yard wearing nothing but Mother's sunglasses overwhelming her tiny face. Some moments were challenging, the four of us trying to learn enough French to order ham sandwiches on the first night of our year-long stay in Paris. Some moments were terrifying, the instant we learned an eleven year old in our town had shot and killed his parents and brother. There is no one left in my circle who lived through these moments with me, no one with whom to share. So I write. Occasionally I string together some words about nature, colorful birds, crimson sunsets, craggy mountains. I try to write about places I've visited on recent trips, moments that excite my senses.

>So little about today.
>My words are for tomorrow
>for the faint rose glow
>climbing above peaks

I must force myself to look ahead, to think about tomorrow's early walk, a quiet moment on the patio with the day's first cup of coffee, the sun rising above the northeast face of the Catalina Mountains.

>for the gold green
>of a willow leaf

Tomorrow I will park myself at the computer desk under the window in the spare bedroom, open the shades, watch verdins fly in and out of the desert willow tree just now popping out its spring leaves.

>   for a glance, a nod
>   for the familiar
>   unfolding.

Always I'm drawn back to the past when I drive along Camino Miraval where my parents lived, or walk past Nugent Hall where my father worked, or eat at the Blue Willow where my sister and I split big breakfasts.

>   We turn our heads
>   to catch a glimpse of someone
>   we know, reach out a hand
>   for a remembered touch

It's only a glimpse, a fleeting presence, a memory gone without a touch.

>   then turn back
>   walk on.

Ahead

*after Georgia O'Keeffe,
"Pedernal 1941-42"*

> A yellow ribbon of trees
> stretches along a river
> we cannot see,

I am on a highway in New Mexico driving south toward Arizona from Iowa. It is April and the last time I will make this trip. My car is loaded with suitcases, boxes, the dog and her paraphernalia, my friend who has come to share driving duties. We have just passed through Albuquerque. Off to the east is the Rio Grande River. I know just where I am.

> traces a path
> we cannot know
> into a future
> we cannot imagine.

Or do I know? I am on a path I have not traveled for decades, making a permanent move into the unknown. Sort of unknown. Certainly I know where I am going, know the city, lived there for awhile in second grade and as a teenager and young adult, have been spending winters there since I retired over a decade ago. But this feels different; this feels like saying good-bye to home. This feels like being a stranger in a strange land.

> A yellow ribbon of trees
> invites us on a journey
> whose destination
> remains a mystery.

The cottonwoods are bursting into bloom along the river leading me south. Their rustle speaks of beginnings, rebirth after a harsh winter in an arid space. The trees say renewal, adventure, change. They awaken me to a life of possibilities, choices. Who among my winter acquaintances will become my friend? Which family member will I discover to be my pillar of strength? Where in my new community will I find a call to help?

A yellow ribbon of trees
beckons.

I follow, open-minded, open-hearted, ready.

Acknowledgments

The following poem/essay hybrids have been previously published: "Ahead" in *Fine Lines* Winter 2020, "At the Sandoz Place" in *Voices from the Plains III* 2019, "Called to Stay" in *Fine Lines* Summer 2019, "Failure" in *The Blue Guitar Magazine* Fall 2021, "For Tomorrow" in *Voices from the Plains IV* 2020, "Keep Searching" in *Stories from the Plains* Fall 2021, "Snow Day" in *Fine Lines* Winter 2022, "Thistle" in *Voices from the Plains III* 2019, and "Travelers" in *What Are Birds* Spring 2020.

The following individual poems have been previously published: "Ahead" in *Unstrung* Summer 2018, "At the Sandoz Place" in *Against the Grain* 1988, "Blaze" in *Unstrung Summer* 2017, "Called to Stay" in *Lyrical Iowa* 2011, "Fathers and Daughters" in *Wingless Dreamer* 2020, "First Steps" in *Sandcutters* 2016, "For Tomorrow" in *Unstrung* Summer 2019, "In Paris" in *Lyrical Iowa* 2007, "Just Lingering" in *Lyrical Iowa* 2012, "Keep Searching" in *Lyrical Iowa* 2010, "On the Path" in *The Weekly Avocet* 2016, "Reflection" in *Sandcutters* 2018, "Restoration" in Janet McMillan Rives, *Into This Sea of Green: Poems from the Prairie* 2020, "Thistle" in *Lyrical Iowa* 2018.

Through the Learning Curve of Tucson, I have benefitted from the help of three excellent teachers. Thanks go to Marge Pellegrino, generator of a million ideas, to Molly McKasson who presented me with the concept of a "woven poem," and to Meg Files for her helpful comments in editing this manuscript.

Janet McMillan Rives was born in Hartford and raised in Storrs, Connecticut. In high school she moved to Tucson, Arizona where she currently lives. She is a graduate of the University of Arizona (B.A.) and Duke University (M.A., Ph. D.) She taught college economics for thirty-five years and retired as Professor Emerita of Economics from the University of Northern Iowa. In addition to writing, her interests include travel, gardening, and golf.

Her love of poetry began during her youth in New England when she discovered the poetry of Robert Frost. She has been reading poetry her entire life and actively writing poetry since the late 1980s. Among her favorite poets are W. S. Merwin, Ted Kooser, Mary Oliver, Naomi Shihab Nye, and Ofelia Zepeda. In addition to being active in small poetry writing groups, she was a member of the Iowa Poetry Association when living in Iowa and is currently a member of The Arizona State Poetry Society and the Tucson Poetry Society. Her poems have appeared in *Lyrical Iowa, Ekphrastic Review, Creosote, Canary, Crosswinds, Sandcutters, The Avocet, Unstrung, The Blue Guitar, Fine Lines,* and in several anthologies. She is the author of two chapbooks—Into *This Sea of Green: Poems from the Prairie* (Finishing Line Press 2020) and *Washed by a Summer Rain: Poems from the Desert* (Kelsay Books 2023).

www.ingramcontent.com/pod-product-compliance
Lightning Source LLC
Chambersburg PA
CBHW020343170426
43200CB00006B/495